A Man's Guide To

Divorce Strategy

Books by David T. Pisarra, Esq.

A Man's Guide To Divorce Strategy

A Man's Guide to Child Custody

A Man's Guide to Domestic Violence

A Man's Guide To Divorce Strategy

By David T. Pisarra, Esq.

Santa Monica, CA

Copyright © 2010 by David T. Pisarra

LIBERO MEDIA

1305 Pico Blvd
Santa Monica, CA 90405

All rights reserved. No part of this publication may be reproduced, stored in a retrieval system, or transmitted, in any form or by any means, electronic, mechanical, photocopying, recording, or otherwise, without the prior permission of the publisher.

ISBN: 978-0-9831635-0-3

The information contained in this book is designed to give an overview and is not a substitute for meeting with a competent family law attorney who can review the full set of facts in any particular case. No warranty is made, express or implied and neither Libero Media nor David T. Pisarra assume any liability in connection with any use or result from reliance on the information contained in this book.

	Lucasville	
364.73	Am	14.95
Pis	Pisarra, David T.	
	A man's guide to divorce strat	

"It's not about bashing women, it's about EMPOWERING MEN."

This series of books is written to empower men to know what their legal rights and responsibilities are. So often I find men have no real idea of what is expected from them, and more importantly, what THEY can expect from the legal system.

As a voice for men, I strive to be
direct, honest, and **clear.**

David T. Pisarra, Esq.

"The woman you married,

is NOT the woman you are divorcing."

~ David T. Pisarra, Esq. ~

A Man's Guide To Divorce Strategy

CONTENTS

- [TWO QUESTIONS EVERY MAN ASKS](#) 1
- [DIVORCE STRATEGY IN A NUTSHELL](#) 5
  - House vs. Boat Discussion 5
  - Alimony 6
  - Alimony and 7
  - the 10 Year Rule 7
  - Pensions 7
  - International Divorce 8
  - Non-Resident Divorce 9
  - Legal Separation 10
  - Breach of Fiduciary Duty 11
  - Dividing Marital Property 11
  - Complex Property Division 12
  - Division of Debts 13
  - Treatment of Debts 13
  - Division of Real Property 14
  - Divorce Dos and Don'ts 17
  - Divorce FAQs 19
  - Divorce Recovery 21

TOP 3 STRATEGIC MISTAKES 23
DOMESTIC VIOLENCE 25
RESTRAINING ORDERS 26
THE REASON FOR TROs IN CUSTODY BATTLES 29
WHY FATHERS NEED TO CONTEST TROs. 30
TROs ARE FOR MEN ALSO ! WOMEN ALSO COMMIT BATTERY. 31
FALSE CHARGES OF 33
DOMESTIC ABUSE 33
PITFALLS OF DO-IT-YOURSELF RESTRAINING ORDERS 34
ASKING THE COURT FOR A RESTRAINING ORDER 34
DEFENDING AGAINST A RESTRAINING ORDER 35

PROPERTY ISSUES 37
SEPARATE PROPERTY DEFINED 37
COMMUNITY PROPERTY DEFINED 40
PROPERTY AND ASSET DIVISION 41
SPOUSAL SUPPORT OR ALIMONY MODIFICATIONS 47
ALIMONY & THE 10 YEAR RULE 49
UNDERPERFORMING AT WORK 50
VOCATIONAL TESTING 51

CHILDREN 55
LEGAL CUSTODY 55
PHYSICAL CUSTODY 56
VISITATION 58

PATERNITY DEFINED 59
RIGHTS OF UNMARRIED PARENTS 61
SUPERVISED VISITATION 63
CHILDREN OF DOMESTIC PARTNERSHIPS 65
CHILDREN'S PREFERENCES IN CUSTODY DISPUTES 65
CREATIVE CHILD CUSTODY AGREEMENTS 66
DETAILS ON VISITATION 67
DEVELOPING A CUSTODY PLAN 68
SPECIAL NEEDS CHILDREN 69
COURT APPOINTED EXPERTS 69
OUT-OF-STATE CUSTODY PROCEEDINGS 71
PARENTAL ALIENATION 72
STEPPED-UP VISITATION 74
UNDERSTANDING CHILD CUSTODY LAWS 75
UNIFORM CHILD CUSTODY JURISDICTION ACT 77
PARENTING PLANS 78

CHILD SUPPORT 79
CHILD SUPPORT DEFENSE 80
CHILD SUPPORT ENFORCEMENT 81
WAGE GARNISHMENTS 81
CHILD SUPPORT GUIDELINES 83
CHILD SUPPORT MODIFICATION 84
DEPARTMENT OF CHILD SUPPORT SERVICES 85
HIGH-EARNER CHILD SUPPORT 85

How to Calculate 87
Child Support 87
Child support & New Mate Income 87
Move-Away Orders 89
Move-Away or Relocation Situations 90

CASE STUDIES 93
DISTRICT ATTORNEY COLLECTION ABUSE 93
PARENTAL ALIENATION – 94
CHILD ABUSE 94
SEXUAL ABUSE ALLEGATIONS AGAINST FATHER 95
INTERNATIONAL CHILD CUSTODY DISPUTE 96
THE HAGUE CONVENTION 96
CHILD ABANDONED BY MOTHER 97
CHILD SUPPORT MODIFICATION 98
PATERNITY DEFENSE 98
DRIVER'S LICENSE RELEASE 99
ABUSE BY DISTRICT ATTORNEY 99
OVERREACHING BY D.A. 100
SPOUSAL SUPPORT FOR HIM 101

THE THREE P'S OF CHILD CUSTODY 103

ABOUT THE AUTHOR 109

A Man's Guide to Divorce Strategy

TWO QUESTIONS EVERY MAN ASKS

Every man wants to know two things,

    1) "What's it going to cost me?" and

    2) "How long will it take?"

Men usually mean, "How much am I going to pay in fees, alimony, child support." Most men don't really care about the house, the china, or the furniture, etc. Which is why the wife usually ends up with all of the material possessions. But just because she wants it, doesn't mean you should give up THE ENTIRE VALUE of it. Let her have the wedding china and the faux leather couch – just make sure that you get half the value when it comes to settling the balance sheet of your marriage.

A Man's Guide to Divorce Strategy

The legal fees charged by your attorney will largely be determined by your ex, and her attorney. You should accept that part of the process of divorce, as her being angry. Frequently spouses fight with each other, through their attorneys, not based on logically well thought out reasons, but to express the anger over the breakup.

This is one of the ways that unscrupulous attorneys take advantage of the situation. They crank up the anger and resentment, knowing that it will result in more money being spent on court appearances, depositions, unending document production demands, forensic accountants, psychologists, parenting coaches, and the list goes on.

Regarding alimony and child support, these amounts are dependent on what you earn, the standard of living that was established while

A Man's Guide to Divorce Strategy

you were married and how much time you have with your child.

The answer to the second question is also dependent on the answer to the first, the more that there is at stake, the longer it can take for a divorce to be processed. The actual legal requirements range from a few days to six months. But until the parties are done fighting, it won't end.

A Man's Guide to Divorce Strategy

A Man's Guide to Divorce Strategy

DIVORCE STRATEGY IN A NUTSHELL

HOUSE VS. BOAT DISCUSSION

Men going through a divorce have a desire to get things over with quickly. This can lead them to making rash decisions such as giving up the house, an asset that can increase in value, for the boat, an asset that will decrease in value each year.

Men need to remember that the decisions they make today will have long term effects on their financial well-being - this is why an attorney who sees beyond the battle of today is crucial to someone in the fog of a divorce.

A Man's Guide to Divorce Strategy

ALIMONY

Alimony, sometimes called Spousal Support, is the ongoing support obligation of one party in a marriage who has been the primary earner. Historically this has been the man, but as times have changed, more and more men, have the right to receive alimony from their ex-wives.

More men are the primary caregiver to the children these days, and if they have sacrificed their careers to be home for the children, they are entitled to alimony in the same way a woman would be.

Many men receive alimony from their ex-wives by being able to prove that they were the primary caregivers, or that they earned less than their spouses, but the standard of living entitled them to spousal support.

A Man's Guide to Divorce Strategy

ALIMONY AND THE 10 YEAR RULE

In America today, a marriage that has lasted more than 10 years is considered to be a marriage of "long duration." What that generally means is that the courts can continue to hold jurisdiction over the parties forever in regards to ordering alimony.

The 10 year rule is why many people will wait out the last years of a bad marriage. They want to ensure that the other party has to provide a lifetime alimony or spousal support award. It is a negotiation ploy that is sometimes used by older women, to make sure they are well taken care of into their golden years.

PENSIONS

Monies earned during marriage are

A Man's Guide to Divorce Strategy

considered Community Property, which means that any contributions to Pensions, 401(k)s, IRAs, or other retirement plans are considered Community Property as well.

Pensions are divided based on the amount of time that a person is married, over the amount of time that a person worked. For example, if a man worked 10 years at MGM Studios, and was married for 2 of those years, the community property interest is 20% (2 out of the 10 years), and so his ex-wife would be entitled to ½ of the 20% (or 10% of the pension).

INTERNATIONAL DIVORCE

Love sees no color and no borders. Married couples who are from two different

A Man's Guide to Divorce Strategy

countries may find themselves in need of a divorce. A divorce issued in one country is, usually, recognized in another jurisdiction. There are some exceptions, but if a divorce is issued in California, it will generally be recognized in all other jurisdictions.

International marriages mean multiple countries and property issues. A court in Kansas will not be able to make orders regarding property in another country, however, it can balance out the division of property by giving one party all the property in Kansas to make up for the property the other person gets in a foreign country.

NON-RESIDENT DIVORCE

If a husband lives in America and the wife lives in a foreign country, the divorce process can be delayed as the court will require that the wife be given notice of the divorce and have an opportunity to appear and ask for her half of the community property. This is especially true if there are children involved.

LEGAL SEPARATION

Legal separation is very similar to divorce, and the process is identical. Property issues, children, and fiduciary responsibilities are dealt with based on the same legal standards, and a judgment is entered such that the parties can live their lives apart.

There are a few reasons to consider a legal separation versus a divorce. Primarily they have to do with health insurance, which can be maintained when legally separated. Armed forces pensions and social security benefits require a ten year period of marriage.

BREACH OF FIDUCIARY DUTY

Husbands owe wives, and wives owe husbands a fiduciary duty to act in the best interests of the marriage. This means that they are not to spend the community property income on frivolous items.

A wife cannot take the bank account and hide the money in her mother's name and a husband can't take the savings account and put it in his girlfriend's name. The court can give the innocent party ALL of the money if they catch someone doing this.

DIVIDING MARITAL PROPERTY

The general rule is that all property acquired during a marriage is community property, and is to be divided equally between the parties. In most marriages this is relatively

A Man's Guide to Divorce Strategy

easy - there is a house, a couple of cars, some tools, her purses, his golf clubs, etc. The only question is how much is it all worth, and to how to divide it so that both parties are treated fairly.

The primary tool used is an "Equalizing Payment." Once everything is accounted for, and the parties agree on what the values are, one party may take the house, and the other party will get a check to balance out the division of marital property.

COMPLEX PROPERTY DIVISION

In large asset cases, where there are multiple properties, stocks, bonds, companies, cars, boats, vacation homes, and other toys, this process can be quite complex. Frequently appraisers, accountants, and business brokers are employed to determine the valuations of the assets.

DIVISION OF DEBTS

When two people are married, their debts are community property also. They are both responsible for the debt incurred and a court is supposed to divide it equally, but there are a few exceptions.

Some debts are not going to be divided, for instance, school loans are assigned to the party who incurred them. This is because it is presumed that the party who has the education will use it to make money in the future.

TREATMENT OF DEBTS

Debts that are jointly owed, like credit cards, department stores, and home mortgages can be divided, or they can be assigned by the parties when they are dividing the community property.

The difficulty for many couples is that one party is the high earner, who qualified for the loan, while the low earner will not be able to repay the debt on their own. In that case, the mortgage holder, the bank, will not let the high earner out of their responsibility to pay back the mortgage.

DIVISION OF REAL PROPERTY

The family home is usually the largest asset to be divided. We have many ways of handling the division. The easiest is to sell the home, but frequently one party wants to hold on to the home, especially if there are children involved. If the wife wants to keep the family home, then sometimes a refinancing of the

A Man's Guide to Divorce Strategy

mortgage is done to put the mortgage in her name and to pay him off. Other times the husband will hold a second mortgage on the property and wait for his money, until the property is sold or refinanced.

If there is real property, such as a vacation home or an apartment building that is producing income, we have other ways of handling these assets. We can change the way that the title is held, so that each party continues to own the property, but in such a way that if one party were to die, it would not get inherited by the ex. Sometimes a property management firm is put in place to ensure an accurate accounting of the income.

A Man's Guide to Divorce Strategy

A Man's Guide to Divorce Strategy

DIVORCE DOS AND DON'TS

"Dos"

1. Speak to a qualified family law attorney.
2. Be Prepared - emotionally, financially and legally.
3. Remember the person you are divorcing, is not the person you married.
4. Protect yourself, YOUR KIDS, and your assets.
5. Pay off YOUR credit cards before you pay off hers.

"Don'ts"

1. **Don't trade your interest in the house, an appreciating asset, for the boat,**

A Man's Guide to Divorce Strategy

which is a depreciating asset. This is the most important concept to learn.

2. Don't pay off all of the debt with Community Property Money, wait until it is divided - you are only responsible for paying off your half of it.
3. Don't move out of the family house if you have children unless it is for your own safety. You're establishing a "status quo" in regards to the children that will handicap you later on visitation and child support.
4. Don't let her seduce you again – it can affect your date of separation and that can affect Alimony !!!

A Man's Guide to Divorce Strategy

DIVORCE FAQS

1) Will I have to pay alimony forever?

That depends on how long you were married, if she is capable of working, and what type of job she can perform. There are many factors that affect this, and no answer is always correct.

2) Will I lose my kids?

Probably not, but understand that there are two types of custody: Legal Custody and Physical Custody. Legal Custody has to do with your right to see your children and make decisions about them. This is difficult to lose, you have to be a bad parent and your ex has to fight you on it. Physical Custody is where they actually live and sleep. Again it is hard to lose

A Man's Guide to Divorce Strategy

ALL physical custody, usually one parent has "Primary" which means the children spend most of their time at that parent's home, and the other parent has visitation.

3) Why do I have to pay alimony?

When two people get married, they establish a standard of living, and usually both are making career sacrifices to build a family. The party who is sacrificing their career to build a home has the right to be compensated, and to have some time to get back on their feet financially and career wise. That is what Alimony is for, to assist people while they work toward support themselves financially.

4) Why doesn't she have to account for the child support I pay?

A Man's Guide to Divorce Strategy

The court assumes that a custodial parent will use the child support paid, for the maintenance and care of the child. This includes things like rent, food, utilities, and clothing. The court's role is to ensure that children are supported in an appropriate manner. Your approval is not required.

DIVORCE RECOVERY

First marriages end in divorce about 70% of the time these days. Most divorces take about a year to complete, from start to finish. As painful as divorce is, most people report being much happier a year after the divorce is over, which means that you will survive this period and come out of it a better, happier person.

Be warned though, people who get into another relationship within 15 months of the breakup, have a much higher chance of another

A Man's Guide to Divorce Strategy

divorce. Those who wait 16 months or more, have a much higher success rate on their second marriages.

Men tend to recover faster from a divorce than women, both emotionally and financially. But that doesn't mean you should give up everything, or even more than half, to get out of the first marriage.

Remember, she may have sacrificed career for your family, you sacrificed time with your family in order to provide for them. A court will not give you more time with your children now to "balance things out." So you might as well at least leave in a good financial position, which will allow you to enjoy the time you have with your children when you do have them.

A Man's Guide to Divorce Strategy

TOP 3 STRATEGIC MISTAKES

1 - Paying off credit card debt.

Paying off credit card debt with community property is a big mistake for men if their ex-wife has a job. If she is working, it is better to split the debt up, and then pay it off with after separation earnings. That way you are only paying off YOUR half of the debt.

2 - Leaving the family home to create peace.

Leaving the family home to "maintain peace" is generally a mistake as you have established a status quo in regards to the children, and you remove the potential for actually working through our emotional pain (often anger).

A Man's Guide to Divorce Strategy

3 - Don't leave anything in the family home – "Take the water from the pool."

Leaving the family home and NOT taking everything you can. You can always give things back, but you will spend thousands of dollars to retrieve items that you could have taken with ease. If there is a lot of fighting going on, you will only make it worse by leaving things you want. All you are doing is creating more topics to fight over.

A Man's Guide to Divorce Strategy

DOMESTIC VIOLENCE

Domestic Violence is a tragedy. It is painful, shameful, damaging psychologically to everyone in the household, especially children who are frequently the innocent observers.

Domestic Violence happens when one person physically attacks another, threatens, harasses, or intentionally disturbs the peace and serenity of the other party.

The true rate of Domestic Violence is hard to quantify as so many incidents of Domestic Violence, go unreported. Men are chronic under-reporters of being abused, for fear of being mocked.

There is a social perception that it is okay for a woman to hit a man, and that he is supposed to just accept it. That is NOT however

A Man's Guide to Divorce Strategy

the law. A man has just as much right, and perhaps more of an obligation, to call the police and have them arrest the perpetrator if he is attacked by his spouse, whether it be his wife, girlfriend, husband or boyfriend.

Anyone who is a victim of Domestic Violence should obtain restraining orders immediately. Men in particular should be aware of how to obtain them, and how important they are in a custody battle over children, as they can and will have a dramatic and long term effect on the rights and availability of visitation.

RESTRAINING ORDERS

Restraining Orders can be obtained in emergency situations by the police when the court system is unavailable - these are called "Emergency Protective Orders." They are issued by a judicial officer who is "on call" and

A Man's Guide to Divorce Strategy

available to the police, after court hours, over weekends, and on holidays.

The more common way to obtain a restraining order is to file a petition under a Domestic Violence Protection Act (DVPA). Each state will generally have a form that is free to file asking the court to restrain a person based on the declaration of the victim. The form requires that a person sign a Declaration under PENALTY OF PERJURY stating the grounds for the issuance of an immediate restraining order.

People frequently lie on declarations in order to get immediate custody of the home, children, and pets. The first restraining order issued is called a Temporary Restraining Order (TRO). It is issued without a court hearing actual testimony and usually the restrained person is not present.

A Man's Guide to Divorce Strategy

In divorce proceedings Temporary Restraining Orders are frequently used to "kick out" one spouse from the home, based on allegations that domestic abuse is occurring. They can be used to require someone to turn in their handguns, stay away from a business they've built, and frequently prevent them from seeing their children.

In most states once a person has been kicked out of their home based on a Temporary Restraining Order, a hearing will be set approximately 20 days later for a full hearing on the merits of the initial order. These hearings can last from 5 minutes to days. They should NOT BE IGNORED.

If you are facing a Temporary Restraining Order, seek legal counsel immediately as the hearing is only a few days away and you need to defend yourself against all charges.

A Man's Guide to Divorce Strategy

THE REASON FOR TROS IN CUSTODY BATTLES

In Child Custody battles, whether as part of a marital dissolution or paternity case, TRO's are frequently used to "kick out" one spouse from the home, and to gain custody of the children, based on allegations that domestic abuse is occurring.

If a person is found by the court to be a Domestic Violence Abuser, which can be based on a statement as simple as "He scared me", they can lose both Legal and Physical Custody of their children. The "victim" will be granted Primary Physical Custody of the children and that will affect visitation.

Supervised visitation is frequently requested and granted in cases where a TRO has been issued. This means that a father will have to have another adult present for him to see his children.

Perhaps most importantly, TRO's make it extremely easy for the "victim" to move to another city or state if they want to, in order to frustrate the ability of the "abuser" to see the children.

WHY FATHERS NEED TO CONTEST TROS.

Once declared an abuser, the presumptions of equal parenting are destroyed. An abuser is considered to be a detriment to the health and well-being of the children and will have to go through a rehabilitation program to comply with court orders, such as anger management classes, parenting classes, and in many cases a 52-week batterer's prevention program.

A Man's Guide to Divorce Strategy

TROS ARE FOR MEN ALSO ! WOMEN ALSO COMMIT BATTERY.

Men are placed in a terrible position in our society. They are told they cannot hit a woman, but that it is okay for a woman to hit a man. Men are told it is 'unmanly' to call the police to "fight your fight" against a woman. Frequently an angry woman will call a man a coward if he attempts to call the police, and an abuser if he defends himself.

The answer is that a man MUST CALL THE POLICE if he is being abused by a woman. It is not a matter of being called a coward, a wimp, a pussy, a fag or a loser. It is the only way he has a chance of winning. If he can prove that he was not the aggressor, which he can do if he is the one who calls the police first, then he has an argument to the judge in court. If he does

A Man's Guide to Divorce Strategy

nothing, he's going to lose. Any woman that is willing to hit a man, and call him a coward, a pussy, a fag, or a loser, will not think twice about committing perjury to win in court.

There's another reason also, protecting the children. If a woman is dangerous, and the man does not take action to protect his children, they could be taken away from BOTH parents by Department of Child Protective Services and he could be found to be a negligent parent because he left the children with a dangerous person.

A Man's Guide to Divorce Strategy

FALSE CHARGES OF DOMESTIC ABUSE

Domestic abuse and domestic violence are the same thing. False charges of domestic abuse or violence are common and in cases where there are no children, a restraining order will be issued and the couple will separate and go on their way. In families with children, the use of false claims of domestic abuse are used as a means to gain an advantage in child custody fights.

Because a "victim" has such a huge advantage in court over an "abuser" in a child custody case, there is a strong motive to put forth false charges in court. If someone wants to gain custody of the children at all costs, they will not think twice about committing perjury.

This is why if you have been served with

A Man's Guide to Divorce Strategy

a restraining order you need to hire a lawyer immediately to defend yourself.

PITFALLS OF DO-IT-YOURSELF RESTRAINING ORDERS

A restraining order can be issued on a declaration signed under penalty of perjury, but the judicial officer who issues the initial restraining order, one that can kick a person out of their home and prevent them from seeing their children, almost never takes testimony for the alleged victim. Most of the time the "abuser" is not present or even aware that a restraining order is being asked for.

ASKING THE COURT FOR A RESTRAINING ORDER

In asking for a restraining order that you have written yourself, you may not ask for enough protection, or you may put statements in your declaration that can be used against you at the hearing on the permanent restraining order. This is why you should always seek an attorney who is experienced in restraining order preparation.

DEFENDING AGAINST A RESTRAINING ORDER

Defending against a restraining order is a highly technical skill and one that requires a lawyer who knows their way around a courtroom and the rules of evidence and how to get to the truth of a case. Defending a restraining order that is based on lies is extremely difficult and is not something that an inexperienced person should attempt.

A Man's Guide to Divorce Strategy

PROPERTY ISSUES

SEPARATE PROPERTY DEFINED

Separate Property is all of the assets that you own before you were married, in some cases it is income from assets you owned prior to marriage. And it is money, stocks, bonds, homes, apartments or businesses that are inherited by you or given to you.

Separate Property will remain separate if you keep it in a separate bank account. However, once you put both separate property and community property into the same bank account, it is generally considered to be a gift, or transmutation in legal terms, to the community. Depending on the circumstances of the deposit, it can be retrieved, but that can be expensive to prove.

A Man's Guide to Divorce Strategy

INHERITANCE

Money and assets that are inherited are considered to be your separate property and in a divorce or dissolution they will be awarded to you by the court, so long as you can prove what was inherited. This will apply to everything that you can account for as an inheritance, whether it comes from your parents, or your 4th cousin three times removed.

GIFTS FROM OTHERS

If someone gives you a gift, it is considered to be your separate property, unless the gift is obviously a gift to the marriage. Thus, if your best friend gives you a fishing rod, it would be considered yours, but if your mom gives you a blender for a wedding gift, it is a gift to the two of you as a married couple and would be considered Community Property.

GIFTS FROM SPOUSE

Gifting applies between spouses also. When you buy your spouse a piece of jewelry it is usually a gift to her from you. You have spent Community Property and by giving it to her, you are giving up your Community Property interest in that jewelry. Sometimes it can be argued that the "gift" was really an "investment" meant for the community to profit from, and for her to enjoy for a period of time. This would apply in cases where the "gift" was something that would be part of an investment portfolio, or business.

If a vintage car dealer let his wife drive a '56 Cadillac that is in her name, he could argue that she was just using the car which was community property. She could argue that because it was her name, it was a gift of community property to her, making it her separate property.

A Man's Guide to Divorce Strategy

COMMUNITY PROPERTY DEFINED

Community property is anything that is acquired during marriage - it can be income from a job or business, a home, boat, vacation home, or the pots and pans that were bought with community property income. The courts try to include everything as Community Property and limit the things that are to be kept separate. The reason for this is that historically a man had an advantage by handling the finances, making the majority of the income and controlling how it was spent. It was felt that if one party had more control it would be easier to hide it, and it would unfairly deny the other person their fair share.

As women have assumed a broader role in society, and have started to earn just as much as men, and have equal or greater control of

A Man's Guide to Divorce Strategy

their finances, the rule continues to be that we try to consider everything as community property. This helps ensure that everyone is on good behavior with being honest about what they make and how much money the couple has.

PROPERTY AND ASSET DIVISION
PROPERTY ISSUES

The general rule is to divide the value equally. To do that we take the market value of the home, subtract the mortgage and costs of sale and divide what's left over. The family home is usually the biggest item that has to be divided. We have many ways of handling the division.

The easiest is to sell the home, but frequently one party wants to hold on to the home, especially if there are children involved.

A Man's Guide to Divorce Strategy

If the wife wants to keep the family home, then either a refinancing of the mortgage is done to put the mortgage in her name and pay him his portion of the equity, or sometimes the husband carries a second mortgage on the property and he waits for his portion of the equity to be paid at a later date.

If there is other real property, like a vacation home or an apartment building that is producing income, there are other ways of handling those properties. We can change the way that title is held, so that each party continues to own the property, but in such a way that if one party die, it doesn't get inherited by the ex. Sometimes a property management firm will be put in place with income producing properties so as to ensure accurate accounting.

A Man's Guide to Divorce Strategy

COPYRIGHTS, TRADEMARKS & PATENTS

Intellectual property issues in divorces are particularly challenging. The works that someone has created may have little or no liquid value at the time of the divorce, but can go on to be very lucrative.

If a book is written during marriage, technically it would be considered Community Property and should properly be divided equally, but if it hasn't been published yet, of what dollar value is it? For the writer who wants to own it and continue to pursue a publishing deal, it may be very valuable, but to the ex-spouse it may be worth nothing, until it gets published. Once published it may produce millions of dollars of value, particularly if it becomes part of a series of books and/or movies.

An idea can be worthless at one time and

A Man's Guide to Divorce Strategy

highly valuable at another. This is why it is very important when dividing intellectual property (copyrights, trademarks and patents) to make sure that the rights are clear and that they account for some future development.

PROTECTING INVESTMENTS

Married couples frequently have investments that require some management, whether it be a family business, an apartment building, or a stock portfolio. Someone has to be aware of what is going on and protect the investment for the community good. When it comes to these items, there is a fiduciary duty to act in the best interests of the community. This means that whoever is in charge of the property will continue to operate it in such a way as to make sure that it is not damaged or impaired while the parties are negotiating for the division of the asset.

A Man's Guide to Divorce Strategy

Sometimes this results in a court order requiring one party to maintain control and keeping the other party away from the business. These type of cases can become very complicated very quickly and involve restraining orders, and emergency petitions, and security bonds.

PROTECTING PROFESSIONAL PRACTICES

A professional practice such as a dentist, doctor, psychotherapist, lawyer, or chiropractor will be awarded to the person who is licensed for that business. The value of that business however can become an issue of dispute as it would be considered Community Property and even though the practice will be awarded to one party, the value of it will be split.

A one person office can be very difficult to value, as the business is only as valuable as the person who is working in it. As the business grows it becomes easier to value because the value is not tied so directly to one person.

PENSIONS, RETIREMENT PLANS, AND QDROS

Any money deposited into a pension, retirement plan, or a 401(k) during marriage is usually considered to be Community Property.

In order for a fair division to happen the court (or more likely the lawyers as this is a pretty straightforward division) will divide the pension, retirement plan, or 401(k) based on the amount of time that an employee is married, over the amount of time that the employee worked. For example, if a man worked 15 years at Baker Mackenzie, and was married for 5 of those years, the community property interest is 33% (5 out of the 15 years), and so his ex-wife would be entitled to ½ of the 33%, or 16.5% of the pension.

Qualified Domestic Relations Orders (QDRO) are orders that are made by a court directing a pension plan on how to divide the retirement income, when it is paid out.

SPOUSAL SUPPORT OR ALIMONY MODIFICATIONS

Spousal Support (Alimony) is the ongoing support obligation of one party in a marriage who has been the primary wage earner. Traditionally this was the husband, but as times change, more and more men, are receiving alimony from their ex-wives.

More men are the primary caregiver to children these days, and if they have sacrificed their careers to be there for the children, they are equally entitled to alimony as a woman would be.

A Man's Guide to Divorce Strategy

Many men today receive alimony from their ex-wives as a consequence of being able to prove that they were the primary caregivers, or that they earned less than their spouses.

Spousal support is supposed to be based on the standard of living that was enjoyed during the marriage. So if a couple lived on a $100,000 a year, and had a vacation home in Colorado where they would go once each season, that is the standard that should be maintained in a post divorce situation. Rarely is there enough money to make that happen in reality.

Divorces are costly and the operating of two family homes is more expensive than when the couple lived in one, thus there is generally less money available for spousal support. Additionally it is supposed to be a flexible situation where the ex enjoys income based on the working spouse's efforts, but if those efforts don't result in the same income, the alimony should be modified or adjusted downward.

Lastly, marital settlement agreements should contain a provision that if a party remarries or co-habitats with a member of the same or opposite sex in a romantic relationship that the alimony terminates. This is a crucial provision and one that a party who is paying, will definitely want to have in the agreement.

ALIMONY & THE 10 YEAR RULE

Here's an example, in California, a marriage that has lasted more than 10 years is considered to be a marriage of "long duration." What that means is that the courts can continue to hold jurisdiction over the parties forever in regards to ordering alimony, it doesn't mean they will, but that they can.

A Man's Guide to Divorce Strategy

This is why many people will wait out the last two years of a bad marriage, just to make sure that the other party has to provide a lifetime alimony or spousal support award. It is a negotiation strategy that is often used by older women, to make sure they are well taken care of into their golden years.

UNDERPERFORMING AT WORK

Many paying spouses think that they can avoid paying spousal support by underperforming at work, this is a mistake and can result in a court ordering an alimony amount that is based upon historical performance. If a top salesperson who normally makes $200,000 a year, suddenly is making only $20,000 a year, and tries to lower their alimony, the court will want to know why there is a sudden drop in income. If there is a verifiable reason, such as the salesperson sold a product that was then outlawed, a court MAY reduce alimony based upon the change in circumstances.

However, if the salesperson was an advertising sales rep for the Los Angeles Times and they haven't lost their job, the court may look at the situation and decide that the paying spouse is underperforming at work, deliberately not working up to their potential, so that they can lower their alimony payments. If a court decides that the loss of income is intentional, they may refuse to lower the alimony.

VOCATIONAL TESTING

Ex-spouses will occasionally claim that they cannot work and should be supported. This will also happen in child support cases, where one party will say that they have no skills, or no

A Man's Guide to Divorce Strategy

jobs are available for them and that is why the child support should be increased.

In all cases where an ex is under an obligation to be self-supporting, and this is most of them, if they are not working, or they are claiming that they cannot work, or cannot find a job, we can ask the court to order that they be tested for vocational abilities. This is a skills test to see what jobs they are suited to perform. Most people can do more than one job, and a vocational test will allow for an objective third party to make a determination as to what type of work a person is capable of performing. Once we've found out that a person has greater vocational skills, it makes the argument that they can't find work harder for them to maintain.

If we find out that a person has a college degree in accounting, then there is no reason they can't find work as a bookkeeper,

A Man's Guide to Divorce Strategy

accounting clerk, warehouse manager, inventory clerk, or a host of other jobs. By showing the judge that there are those jobs available, the judge can then impute income to the ex, AS IF they had that job. A judge cannot make someone get a job, but a judge can treat them as if they had the income from the work.

A Man's Guide to Divorce Strategy

CHILDREN

LEGAL CUSTODY

Legal Custody is the concept of what rights you have in making decisions for your children's life, and in knowing what is going on in their life. Legal custody means being able to see school records, medical records, choosing what school they go to, and giving consent for medical treatment.

Legal Custody also means the ability to get a passport and travel with the children.

Usually both parents share Legal Custody as a natural part of being a parent. If you are listed on the birth certificate, you would normally automatically have Legal Custody.

To lose Legal Custody, a court must make a ruling that it is not in the best interests of the child for you to have a contributing voice in their upbringing. This is not something that courts do without a significant proof that a parent would be a detriment to the child's life. Frequently the loss of legal custody is a consequence of alcohol or drug abuse, sexual abuse, domestic violence or abandonment.

PHYSICAL CUSTODY

Physical Custody means having the children present with you when you travel. It is the time when they sleep over at your house, and you feed, clothe and house them.

Physical Custody is very much a matter of practicality and logistics. This is the reason that so many fathers do not share equally in the division of physical custody. It is simply not practical for many different reasons, the most common of which is the fact that a father has a

A Man's Guide to Divorce Strategy

job that interferes with his ability to be present for his child.

It is the trap that men are caught in, they are expected to be a good provider during a marriage, and that means they have to work a lot. When the marriage ends, they are expected to continue to provide, but that means that they don't have the time to spend with the children, to shuttle them to soccer games and girl scouts and all the activities that the children have. Many fathers would gladly give up working so hard to have more time, but they are bound to provide alimony and child support based on their prior incomes and now they can't reduce that income.

In two-income families where mother and father both work outside the home, the reason that fathers again lose physical custody is because they generally have moved out, so as to

A Man's Guide to Divorce Strategy

cause the least disruption to the children, but in doing so, they have created a family structure that a court will not change unless it is shown that mom is unstable or a bad parent, or some other change of circumstance that is significant.

VISITATION

Reasonable visitation is due to every paren. What this means for the non-custodial parent is that they will have some amount of time given to them to be with the children, usually it is every other weekend and a weeknight dinner. This was decided many years ago as a "workable" situation as has become a default for the courts. It does not have to be that way, but if you and your ex cannot agree on a different arrangement, it is the most likely scenario a judge will give you.

Most holidays will be shared, either by

alternating them, where one parent takes the odd years and the other parent takes the even years, or the day is split with morning and afternoon sessions. Some holidays and special days are automatically given to you, as a father you can expect visitation on Father's day, as well as your birthday. The child's birthday will generally alternate from year to year.

PATERNITY DEFINED

Paternity actions decide that there is a legal relationship between child and a man. They can be filed by either the mother or the father to determine and establish rights and responsibilities in regards to a child.

Traditionally they were filed by women seeking child support from a man for the child. As society has changed and more people are having children outside of marriage, men are

A Man's Guide to Divorce Strategy

starting to file paternity actions to secure their rights to their children. As more and more men become primary caregivers, and it becomes more commonplace for a man to raise a child, these types of cases are becoming everyday occurrences.

We have handled many paternity actions, on both sides, where mom was seeking to get child support from dad, and where dad was seeking to get custodial time and visitation with his child.

If there is a question as to the actual paternity, a genetic test can be ordered and performed that will provide the court with 99% certainty as to whether a particular man is or is not the father of a child.

A Man's Guide to Divorce Strategy

RIGHTS OF UNMARRIED PARENTS

Unmarried parents of a child are in a different legal position than married couples. The mother is automatically granted Legal and Physical Custody of a child upon birth because it is clear that she is the mother.

An unmarried father has to assert his rights because it is not immediately clear that he is the father. Once a child is born, if he is certain that he is the father, he can sign the birth certificate and the Voluntary Declaration of Paternity which will act as a judgment of paternity within 60 days if he does not revoke it. When those two items are signed and recorded he becomes the father legally and will have a legal right to both Legal Custody and Physical Custody.

Just because he has the right to both

A Man's Guide to Divorce Strategy

Legal Custody and Physical Custody does not mean that it will happen automatically, that is why he must file a paternity action. A Paternity Action allows a court to order visitation for the father, and enforce his rights to his child's medical, dental, educational and religious information.

CHILD VISITATION

Reasonable visitation is due to every parent, what this means for the non-custodial parent is that they will have some amount of time given to them to be with the children, usually it is every other weekend and a weeknight dinner. This was decided many years ago as a "workable" situation and has become a default for the courts. It does not have to be that way, but if you and your ex cannot agree on a different arrangement, it is the most likely scenario a judge will give you.

A Man's Guide to Divorce Strategy

Most holidays will be shared, either by alternating them, where one parent takes the odd years and the other parent takes the even years, or the day is split with morning and afternoon sessions. Some holidays and special days are automatically given to you, as a father you can expect visitation on Father's day will be your as well as your birthday. The child's birthday will generally alternate from year to year.

SUPERVISED VISITATION

Supervised visitation is ordered when one parent asks for it, and the court believes that the other parent is dangerous, unstable or requires supervision to ensure the child's safety. There are both professional monitors and family monitors allowed. Professional monitors can be beneficial for the parent who is being

A Man's Guide to Divorce Strategy

supervised, as the professional can provide notes and reports to the court that are unbiased.

Supervision is an uncomfortable fact for many men. It is viewed by them as humiliating, demeaning, belittling and shameful. These feelings are understandable, but usually the fact of supervision is more of an indication of the mother's state of mind, than it is the danger that the father presents.

Properly used, the fact that there is an objective third person to report to the court, can be useful, if the reports come back showing how devoted, attentive, and wonderful a father the man is, and how paranoid, overly protective, and alienating the mother is.

CHILDREN OF DOMESTIC PARTNERSHIPS

Children born during a Domestic Partnership are entitled to the same protections and rights as children born during a marriage. There are some technical issues regarding adoption by the non-biological parent and how that will affect a visitation and child custody plan.

CHILDREN'S PREFERENCES IN CUSTODY DISPUTES

In general a child is not expected, and frequently not allowed, to communicate what their preferences for custody are. The reason for this is to prevent one parent from trying to lobby for custody over the other parent. Many judges will not read letters from the child, no matter how old they are, as a matter of policy. The reason is to prevent the children being put in the middle of the parent's dispute.

However, some judges will read a letter from a child, if they are old enough and if the judge feels that it was not a coerced letter. In some states, a child may be emancipated at the age of 12, consequently some judges will use that as a starting age from which they will start to get information from the child.

CREATIVE CHILD CUSTODY AGREEMENTS

There are no real limits on what you and the other parent can come up with in terms of child custody. It is very dependent on your ability to work together. We have clients who alternate the child every week, others do every other day, some do living situations where the children stay in the house and the parents are

A Man's Guide to Divorce Strategy

the ones who rotate in and out of the house.

It is all a matter of negotiation, so long as you stay away from the judge.

DETAILS ON VISITATION

Visitation is crucial for your relationship with your children. If you are the non-custodial parent, meaning you do not have the children the majority of the time, you need to A) be sure to use all the visitation time you were given either by the judge or in your agreement, and B) Keep a record of what you use, and how you use it.

The value of a Dad's Diary is crucial if you ever get into a fight with your ex over how much you really see your children. Frequently moms like to say that "he never uses the time he's got" as a way to increase their child support. If you need to prove that you actually saw your child you must have a record of what you did, on what day, and be able to show the judge and your lawyer something to support your claims.

DEVELOPING A CUSTODY PLAN

The hardest part for most fathers is the realization that their career obligations interfere with the custody that they would like to have with their children. The reality is that a custody plan has to consider the actual schedule of a child, the work schedule of both parents and the current living situation.

If the family is still under one roof, there is still time to plan and work out a schedule that will be to the father's and children's advantage. If dad is out of the family home, it is going to be very hard to change the custody arrangement.

SPECIAL NEEDS CHILDREN

Special needs children require a much more thorough custody plan and depending on the severity of their needs, support from the parents may continue past the age of majority, when most support ends.

School plans and housing can be difficult to deal with when the parents have a special needs child, and the parents are not agreeing on what is in the best interests of the child. This may lead to the request by one or both parents for a 730 Evaluation.

COURT APPOINTED EXPERTS
CUSTODY EVALUATIONS

In California, Evidence Code §730 allows a court to appoint an expert to give the court additional information and an outside, objective

A Man's Guide to Divorce Strategy

determination of what is happening when the court has either conflicting testimony between the parties, or the situation is such that additional information would help the judge make a ruling. All states have a similar provision for the court to appoint experts.

A 730 Evaluation is usually a long, difficult and emotional process that involves the family being interviewed by a psychologist over several sessions, both individually and in group settings. At the end of the evaluation process a report is generated by the psychologist or social worker for the court to review, and recommendations for custody and visitation.

Properly handled, a 730 Evaluation can be a huge benefit for a father who is fighting false charges or who has an ex who is highly volatile and making co-parenting difficult. If a good expert is hired, one who is highly experienced and has great skill at determining when someone is lying, then the evaluation can be very beneficial.

These are not cheap. A 730 Evaluation can cost from $5,000 and there is no upper limit on what can be spent, though generally they are between $5,000 and $10,000.

OUT-OF-STATE CUSTODY PROCEEDINGS

If you have a custody determination in one state, and live in another, you should either arrange to have the case transferred to the new jurisdiction or be prepared to have the custody hearings held in the original state. The out of state rulings can be enforced in the state you and or the children live.

This is particularly true when it comes to the enforcement of Child Support Awards. The

A Man's Guide to Divorce Strategy

law allows for a Los Angeles Court through the District Attorney's office to enforce a judgment from Arizona when it comes to the collection of Child Support. But it will NOT hear or do anything about the custody and visitation, if you want to change that and get more time with your children.

PARENTAL ALIENATION

Parental Alienation is a heartbreaking situation. When one parent, usually an angry mother, attempts to cut the other parent out of the child's life by subtly and sometimes not so subtly alienating the affections of the child for the parent. This is a very difficult situation to prove to a court, and there is much controversy over whether or not it even exists as a psychological condition.

The American Psychological Association

A Man's Guide to Divorce Strategy

is reviewing the data, and is expected to decide that in the upcoming Diagnostic and Statistical Manual (DSM) if there will be such a diagnosis, and if so, what factors must be present to determine if a parent is either the perpetrator or victim of Parental Alienation.

We have fought these cases, and won, but they are painful, time consuming cases because of their subtlety.

Parental Alienation frequently hides behind a mask of "concerned parent" but its effect is to make the child feel unsafe around the alienated parent – which is child abuse.

Here is an example of Parental Alienation and how it can look like Mom is just being concerned: "Janey, remember, when you're at Daddy's you can always call me and I'll come get you if you don't feel good." That is setting

Mom up as a rescuer, and saying that Dad's house is not safe for Janey to be sick in. It paints Dad as less than a good parent by showing Janey that Mom has to always be ready to come and pick up the pieces when Dad fails.

STEPPED-UP VISITATION

The development of a child from a vulnerable, totally dependent newborn to an independent teen, requires varying degrees of visitation time with the father. While the baby is breastfeeding the father is not considered an essential part of the child's life. Once the child reaches the point of eating food, the father can take on a more active role in the development of the child.

Fathers who want to be an active part in their child's lives will find that they can receive more and more visitation, up to a 50% split, if they have the availability, but it will come in a stepped up fashion. At first a newborn's father may have only a 4-hour visit on a Saturday, then more time, then overnights, then blocks of days.

This same concept of stepped up visitation also applies to fathers who have been absent from a child's life and want to reunite. If a child does not have an established relationship with the father, the court will require a "Reunification Plan" that uses greater and greater blocks of time to allow a child to adjust to the new relationship with a parent they do not know well.

UNDERSTANDING CHILD CUSTODY LAWS

Child custody law and decisions are the most difficult to explain to people who don't eat, live, and breathe them. They are

A Man's Guide to Divorce Strategy

heartbreaking decisions by someone who doesn't have to live with the results. They are made by judges who have limited information and in most cases are overworked and trying to do what is best for a child that they don't know personally.

Child custody battles are hard fought and usually have no winners. The cases turn on a few facts and what looks like a slam dunk case can turn out to be a dead bang loser with just one or two facts perceived differently.

In some areas of the law, like criminal, there are clear, black and white rules. In Family Law and in Child Custody in particular, everything is a constantly evolving shade of grey.

For example, when a court looks at a parent who chronically abuses alcohol, but has no criminal record such as a DUI, that fact may carry little weight. But another parent who occasionally smokes marijuana could be put through a series of supervised visitations based solely on the request of the other parent who provides a declaration that there is marijuana smoking going on.

UNIFORM CHILD CUSTODY JURISDICTION ACT

The Uniform Child Custody Jurisdiction and Enforcement Act (UCCJEA) is what determines whether or not a particular state can hear a case involving a child, based upon where that child has lived just prior to the filing of the case.

The UCCJEA allows for a state to take Temporary Jurisdiction over a child if there is an allegation of child abuse or domestic violence, otherwise the court must defer to the appropriate court. This is a highly technical area of the law, and most people are not qualified to interpret it without an attorney.

PARENTING PLANS

Parenting plans are those agreements made between the parents in regards to child custody, child visitation, holidays, schooling, religious training, extra-curricular activities, and all other aspects of raising a child.

Court ordered mediation is usually the place where parenting plans first get negotiated, if the parties can agree on some or all of the topics, the parenting plan will be written up and then entered as a judgment that will become enforceable by the court and the police.

CHILD SUPPORT

Child support is money that is paid to contribute to the expenses necessary for the maintenance and upbringing of a child. It is based on many factors, the time that the parents share the child, the income levels of each parent, the age of the child, the number of children involved, other children from other relationships etc.

Child support can be decided between mother and father on a very casual basis and the court need not be involved, or it can be a very specific, hard fought battle involving wage garnishments, vocational testing of parents to determine if they are underperforming, and asset searches to determine if money is being hidden.

A Man's Guide to Divorce Strategy

The hard part for men to accept is that while their finances and lifestyles are open to exploration and examination by the courts, how the money is spent by Mom is completely untouchable. The court will not consider what mom is doing with the money, whether it goes for facials or food is not the court's concern. Men cannot make mom do an accounting, but mom can make dad do an accounting to prove that he is paying his child support, and that he is paying the correct child support amount.

CHILD SUPPORT DEFENSE

Child support is a fact of life for fathers, but that doesn't mean that it is a blank check for mom. The mother of a child can file an action for child support and she can claim that the father makes $10,000 a month, and if he doesn't appear in court to defend that, the judge may make a child support order based on mom's statements, which are under penalty of perjury.

It is crucial that a man defend himself in a child support case. It is also crucial that child custody and visitation be addressed to make sure that dad is getting as much visitation as possible with his child, as that will affect how much support is awarded to mom. You cannot change visitation in a District Attorney's Child Support Case, so be sure that a paternity case is opened and that an Order To Show Cause hearing is filed every time that mom wants to increase the child support.

CHILD SUPPORT ENFORCEMENT WAGE GARNISHMENTS

Enforcement of a child support award can be done casually between the parties, where dad writes a check each week, or month.

A Man's Guide to Divorce Strategy

It is absolutely essential, that dad write a check or make an electronic transfer to mom. Never use cash. EVER. NO CASH EVER. Dads have to be able to prove that they have paid their child support, otherwise they may end up having to pay it twice.

If you come to a lawyer's office and say, "I paid my child support." The first question asked will be "How?" It is recommended that you always have a means of proof available.

If you fall behind in your payments of child support, your driver's license, realtors license, or other professional license can be suspended until you get current or make a repayment plan.

Wage Garnishments are another area where men feel humiliated, embarrassed, shameful and guilt-ridden about their child support. This is normal, but it is not an attack on them of them as men, in fact, it makes it much easier to prove that you have paid your child support. Rather than fight the garnishment, most men should embrace it as a way of proving to the court and to the world that they are taking their responsibility seriously. Plus, it's one less check you have to write, and really, do you want to be writing her a check each month?

CHILD SUPPORT GUIDELINES

The guideline support is based on a formula that is so complex only a computer can determine what the right number is. However, the rule of thumb is 25% of your GROSS income as a guesstimate of the amount of child support you will pay.

There are online sources for you to figure out what you think it will be, but the best way is

A Man's Guide to Divorce Strategy

to meet with an attorney who has the Dissomaster program in California, or your state.

CHILD SUPPORT MODIFICATION

Child Support is always modifiable, and that means that if you get a promotion your ex can file a motion to have the child support increased. But it also means that if you lose your job you need to file a motion immediately to have your support reduced based on being unemployed.

Generally if nothing changes, a court will not modify your child support, but in general you can be brought to court every six months to confirm that you are paying the correct amount of money.

A Man's Guide to Divorce Strategy

DEPARTMENT OF CHILD SUPPORT SERVICES

In most states, the Department of Child Support Services handles the enforcement of child support if the mother has opened a case with them. That means that they can place a wage garnishment on you, and can take your tax return if there is an unpaid child support amount.

The Department of Child Support Services website has a child support calculator that you can use to determine what the state guidelines are for you, based on your income level and the amount of visitation you have with your child.

HIGH-EARNER CHILD SUPPORT

Child support is meant to maintain a child in fairly even living environments. The

A Man's Guide to Divorce Strategy

reason for this is that the courts don't want one parent, who may earn substantially more than the other parent, to try to win the love and affection of the child by buying toys and gifts.

This means that the court will look to both parties income and try to make a child support award based on what is needed to equalize the living environments. What this means is that if one parent is a high earner and the other parent is an average earner, the court may deviate from the Guideline support awards and award a sum of money that is much higher than the computer program would come up with, or it may reduce the amount that the Guideline support would indicate if there are factors that would result in an absurd amount of money being paid.

HOW TO CALCULATE CHILD SUPPORT

Calculating Child support requires a complex computer program, and even then, sometimes the court will ignore the results if they are unfair, or are overly generous. This is another one of those many grey areas in family law, the Guideline Child Support awards are a starting point, but if your situation is different for some reason you should speak to an attorney to determine what is the most realistic result.

CHILD SUPPORT & NEW MATE INCOME

In some cases, though not most, a new spouse's income can be used as a factor in child support calculations. Generally, the courts want to know what the actual parent's income is, so

A Man's Guide to Divorce Strategy

that they can make a decision based upon that.

If there is a special needs child involved, the new spouse's income may be a factor, particularly if the primary custodial parent cannot work while caring for the special needs child.

MOVE-AWAY ORDERS

Move-Away cases are heartbreaking. When one parent has a desire to move, and they have custody of a child, they need to file a motion with the court to get permission to move the child's residence, unless the other parent will agree in writing to a modification.

The usual reason for these move-aways is the need for work, or a new relationship. In either case, a court cannot restrain the parent from moving, they have a Constitutional right to move. The court CAN restrain the child from being moved.

Once a motion is filed, the court will order an evaluation of the custody, which can be either a short or "fast track" evaluation. This can be only a few hours, or a full 730 Evaluation depending on if the parents have the money to

A Man's Guide to Divorce Strategy

fund the battle and the evaluation.

In the "up is down, and black is white" world of child custody, the better the parent's relationship is, in terms of working with each other for child custody, the more likely it is the court will allow the child to move. The reason here is that the moving parent will continue to work with the non-moving parent and help the relationship between the child and staying parent.

Additionally, if there are siblings involved the move is more likely to be granted as courts will almost never split up the children, even if they are only half-siblings.

MOVE-AWAY OR RELOCATION SITUATIONS

Move-Away or Relocation situations usually involve mom wanting to move for a

A Man's Guide to Divorce Strategy

better job or a new boyfriend. Sometimes they are used by mom as a way to increase the parental alienation of the father, and are masked with the "new job" or "new boyfriend" cover. Courts will almost always grant these move away requests, though they can put some serious restrictions and requirements in place.

Frequently the parent staying behind can have large blocks of time with the child, such as all the spring, winter, and summer vacations. Or the moving parent may have to bear the burden of most of the traveling costs.

Every situation presents different obstacles and opportunities in move away cases. There are a many factors that go into whether the judge will allow the move away to happen, but generally the judge's job is to make sure that visitation will continue, because in the end, the parent has a constitutional right to move.

A Man's Guide to Divorce Strategy

This is why you should always meet with an experienced attorney to discuss your options.

CASE STUDIES

CHILD SUPPORT & VISITS

Greg B. – We represented this man against an ex-wife who wanted to prevent him from seeing his son, so that she could receive an increased Child Support award. We were victorious in not only keeping his support low, but in increasing his visitation with his son through the crucial pre-teen years.

DISTRICT ATTORNEY COLLECTION ABUSE

Curtis M. - Here we represented our client against the District Attorneys office for a back child support collection matter in which he had fully paid all of his support, but the DA's office continued to collect surplus funds that the ex was no longer entitled to.

PARENTAL ALIENATION – CHILD ABUSE

John B. – For this father, we had to fight to prove that the mother was not only an unfit mother, but that she was physically abusing their daughters, and engaging in extensive parental alienation and emotional abuse of the children.

It took a lot of work, but we were able, after several hearings (Orders to Show Cause - "OSCs") to make the judge see that the father had the more stable, loving and attentive environment for the children to be living in.

A Man's Guide to Divorce Strategy

SEXUAL ABUSE ALLEGATIONS AGAINST FATHER

Doug G. – For this super devoted dad, we had to fight to prove that the mothers multiple allegations of sexual molestation were false. By agreeing to a full psychological evaluation (Family Code §730) we were able to provide the court with an outside, independent, and unbiased opinion of the father's fitness.

The court agreed, and stated that if Mom decided to "move away" from the state of California, the child's primary custody would transfer to Dad. This was a major win for this devoted dad who loves his child, and his little girl, who gets to keep her daddy.

A Man's Guide to Divorce Strategy

INTERNATIONAL CHILD CUSTODY DISPUTE

THE HAGUE CONVENTION

Henry W. – For this father, who was a primary caregiver the majority of his young daughter's life, we continued to demonstrate to the court that the mother was not only an unfit mother, due to her chemical dependency issues, but as she was living in another country, could not provide for regular and ongoing visitation.

In this case, Mom had abducted the child twice, and had a history of border jumping, to avoid letting Dad have visitation. After a period of abandonment by Mom, she decided she wanted to be a loving mother. It had been six years since she had seen her child, so the court provided a reunification program before allowing Mom to see her child. We fought this case under the Hague Convention and UCCJEA rules for child custody. We were able to place enough speed bumps on Mom that no damage was done to the child's emotional well-being.

International custody cases are very difficult and expensive. They can also be some of the most heartbreaking, if there are two good parents.

CHILD ABANDONED BY MOTHER

Raul C. – Representing the father, who had full custody of his son after mom abandoned him, we protected his rights and secured a custody plan that allowed his son the stable, and secure home life that he enjoyed with his father. Mom was allowed only a visitation schedule.

CHILD SUPPORT MODIFICATION

John W. – A short term relationship became a 19 year drama for this man who fathered children with a woman who was using the children to extract support. We held the line on keeping the support amounts low and in line with what the children really needed.

PATERNITY DEFENSE

John Q. – This alleged father came to us after he was served with paperwork demanding that he start paying child support. He claimed that the kids weren't his, so we defended. The initial DNA tests results showed it was not his kid.

DRIVER'S LICENSE RELEASE

Frank S. – Dad had fallen behind on his child support payments, so the Department of Motor Vehicles, at the request of the Department of Child Support Services, suspended his driving privileges. This prevented him from working so that he could make the money, to pay his child support. We appeared in court and were able to work out a release of the Driver's License and a reasonable payment plan that allowed Dad to get back on track.

ABUSE BY DISTRICT ATTORNEY

Cal P. – Another case of loving father who fell behind in his child support payments. His records were not clean and orderly and we had to do a full accounting going back years to find that he had actually overpaid. It was a long battle with the District Attorney, Child Support

Services, and a vindictive, greedy mom, but we won.

OVERREACHING BY D.A.

Keith A. – In yet another horror story about the District Attorney's Office and the Child Support Services incompetence, this Dad, who made all of his child support payments, had his tax refunds, and his bank accounts taken by child support authorities when they "mistakenly" erased the record of all of his payments. They took $25,000 of his money, not once, but TWICE, because of their errors.

It took many hearings and full accountings, but we were able to get all the money returned and the matter cleared up.

SPOUSAL SUPPORT FOR HIM

John D. – Against this high income earning wife we were able to recover a sizable spousal support agreement for our client. This was what we call a 'Mani-mony' case. The ex-wife had to pay spousal support. It took some effort, and some hard nosed tactics, but we were able to negotiate a very high spousal award.

A Man's Guide to Divorce Strategy

A Man's Guide to Divorce Strategy

THE THREE P'S OF CHILD CUSTODY

I believe that parents should be forced to take an equal division of time in their children's care. Fathers should be required by law to take their children 50% of the time.

Mothers frequently withhold their children from the fathers based on the false perception that they are not nurturing enough. Courts tend to support this canard and the only way we will be able to change it, is by men fighting for custody. It is happening more, and as the studies are beginning to show, men are just as capable of being loving and nurturing parents as women. They simply have been denied the opportunity for too long. It's a similar argument that

A Man's Guide to Divorce Strategy

feminists make when it comes to the workplace and equal pay.

The alienating behavior is commonly masked as mom being "protective" – it's bunk. We see this type of controlling behavior is all too often in our practice, and it is a detriment to the father/child bonding relationship.

When a child is only a few months old, they may need the mother for breastfeeding, but even that is no excuse for a father to be denied solo parenting time. Frequently the mom claims that the father is not a good parent, or too immature, or too uneducated to provide for a newborn. Those are weak arguments at best and disingenuous at worst. If a man is old enough to father a child, to be required to pay child support, then he should be able to take up the mantel of parenting.

A Man's Guide to Divorce Strategy

Today, as it stands, fathers who want to obtain, or increase, their visitation and custody orders need to keep in mind the following: **Proximity, Paperwork, and Persistence**. These can make or break your chances of getting the orders issued by the judge. Most fathers start out a custody case at a disadvantage. When dad moves out, the children are left with mom, and that becomes the way the court is inclined to keep the situation. The moment that dad moves out of the family home, is the moment that mom gains an advantage in child custody hearings.

Here's why, the courts don't want to upset the children's living environment. They focus on keeping the child stable, and that means in their historical home.

So how then does a man recover from the mistake of moving out of the house? He must show to the court that he can effectively parent

A Man's Guide to Divorce Strategy

the child, with as little disruption to the child's routine as possible.

PROXIMITY

This means how far or close dad lives to the child's home and school. This is a major factor in increasing, or acquiring, custody and visitation. The closer dad is to the home and school, the more easily he can be present for the child, and the courts give this great weight. If the choice is for a child to be in a car for five minutes getting from mom's home to school or a 25 minute drive from dad's home, the court is going to prefer mom's home. It is also more likely that the child's friends and social network are close to the school they attend, which is a factor for the court.

A Man's Guide to Divorce Strategy

PAPERWORK

Cases are won or lost on documentation. Dads should keep a Calendar or a Diary of all the time that they are with their child. In any contested case, Mom has something that she will use to show the court how little time Dad spends with the kids.

A simple calendar which shows the days that Dad took his child, and what they did on those days can make all the difference for a change in custody. If Dad keeps the receipts for what he did with his child, it will allow his lawyer to prove that he took the child to see the movie "Cars" on a day when Mom says he didn't visit. This is a crucial credibility issue, and one that with a little bit of work by dad, can yield big gains. The court will see that dad is truthful, and that goes a long way towards winning the

A Man's Guide to Divorce Strategy

credibility wars, which can lead to more time with his child.

PERSISTENCE

The biggest factor that effects whether or not a Dad will win more visitation or even equal custody, is his ability to come back, time and time again. The successful Dad in family court, is the Dad who never gave up, and is willing to do whatever it takes, no matter how difficult it is, or how long it takes, to prove to the court that he wants, and is capable of being a loving, attentive and present father. The successful Dad who wants to increase his custody and visitation, will live close, keep good records, and never give up when dealt a bad hand. Society is changing, and as more men are the primary parent, it will become easier for all fathers to have the custodial time and visitation they want with their children.

A Man's Guide to Divorce Strategy

ABOUT THE AUTHOR

David Pisarra has been practicing Family Law in the southern California counties of Los Angeles, Riverside, Orange, Ventura and San Diego since 1998. He has wide experience in Divorces, Child Support, Child Custody, Paternity, Alimony / Spousal Support, and Domestic Violence cases. He has represented both men and women, straight people and gay people successfully.

Mr. Pisarra has sought increases in Alimony, and also termination of Spousal Support orders. His firm believes that testing the supported spouse for their ability to work, called vocational testing, is underused and that many paying spouses could reduce their alimony by finding out that the supported spouse could work or should at least have some responsibility to earn an income.

Mr. Pisarra has represented many fathers in paternity cases, which is a growing area as more people are having children out of wedlock. Fathers have both rights and

A Man's Guide to Divorce Strategy

responsibilities to their children. Whether or not the child is planned, the dad has an obligation to be there for his children. It is always in the man's best interest to confirm that he is the father and if he is, to take responsibility and have an active role in the child's life.

Divorce is a painful process, but having an experienced attorney to help guide you through the mountains of paperwork, and more importantly the emotional rollercoaster ride is crucial to making sure that you leave a marriage with an equal share of the assets.

Lucasville
364.73 Am   14.95
Pis   Pisarra, David T.
         A man's guide to divorce strat